SURVIVING
SIGNALBOXES

SURVIVING SIGNALBOXES

FROM THE GOLDEN AGE
OF BRITISH RAILWAYS

DAVID HUCKNALL

SUTTON PUBLISHING

First published in 2000 by
Sutton Publishing Limited · Phoenix Mill
Thrupp · Stroud · Gloucestershire · GL5 2BU

British Library Cataloguing in Publication Data
A catalogue record for this book is available from the British Library.

ISBN 0-7509-2476-4

Endpapers: Canterbury West signalbox, see pages 118–19.
Frontispiece If ever a signalbox deserved the description 'surviving', it is Eastfield at Peterborough seen here in 1997. It has an incongruous look, hemmed in on one side by the East Coast Main Line and on the other by the complex layout of sidings that make up Peterbrough Yards. In 1926, some twenty-two signalboxes controlled railway activities around Peterborough. By 1977, when Peterborough power signalbox became fully operational, only three 'boxes (at Doncaster, Peterborough and Kings Cross) controlled 156 miles of the East Coast Main Line and Peterborough PSB had assumed responsibility for a large number of local boxes. In this photograph, the entrance-end elevation of Eastfield cabin is shown from Westwood bridge. See also page 78. (*15 June 1997; DJH*)

ACKNOWLEDGEMENTS

It gives me great pleasure to acknowledge the help and assistance given to me in the preparation of this book. My particular thanks to my wife Susan and son Philip who, together with Renate McCarron, typed the manuscript with efficiency and accuracy.

I am also indebted to everyone who has assisted me in obtaining material for this book. Thanks are particularly due to Ivor Lloyd, the Signalling Manager at Worcester, Lawrence James at St Blazey and those signalmen who were kind enough to invite me into their 'boxes. I should also like to express my appreciation to Matt Jukes of ABP, Immingham and Mr K. Burgess of Crosfield Ltd who allowed me to visit the sites under their control.

Finally, I must acknowledge those members of the Signalling Record Society who have helped me at various times. The Society was founded in 1969. It exists for those who have an interest in the history and operation of railway signalling in the British Isles and overseas. Details of membership can be obtained from the Secretary, The Signalling Record Society, 51 Queensway, Wallasey, Merseyside CH45 4PZ.

David Hucknall
Alresford 2000

Typeset in 10/12 pt Palatino.
Typesetting and origination by
Sutton Publishing Limited.
Printed and bound in England by
J.H. Haynes & Co. Ltd, Sparkford.

CONTENTS

INTRODUCTION

In the early 1900s, there were 12,000 signalboxes in use on Britain's railway system. Indeed, from the 1890s through to the 1950s, apart from the removal of some intermediate 'boxes, things were, numerically, relatively stable. Even as late as 1959, British Railways' Southern Region route from Southampton to Weymouth, for example, was still controlled by thirty-five signalboxes.

During the 1960s, several resignalling schemes were carried out in conjunction with modernisation programmes such as the Euston–Manchester/Liverpool electrification. These, together with line closures, a downturn in traffic and a desire to reduce staff levels, brought about a drastic fall in signalbox numbers. By 1970, about 4,000 survived. Signalling Record Society data (see P. Kay, *The Railway Magazine*, *146*, 39 (2000)) on the number of 'boxes abolished each year from 1977 to 1988 show that, during this period, about 100/year were being removed. By 1988, only 1,445 signalboxes remained in service. At this rate, the disappearance of the signalbox would now be imminent, probably to be replaced by a few Integrated Electronic Control Centres (IECC) in which television screens show unmanned level crossings tens of miles away.

Obviously, this has not happened. After 1988, the rate of abolition began to slow and slowed markedly in some years. For example, Kay's article indicates that the average number of closures for 1992–6 was thirty 'boxes/year. Certainly, since Railtrack assumed responsibility for infrastructure, closures have generally declined. Some projects, however, such as EROS – Efficiency through Rationalisation of Signalboxes – have dramatically reduced signalbox numbers in some areas. For example, phase 1 of EROS was responsible for the removal of thirty-six signalboxes, predominantly around Worksop, Barnsley and Castleford.

Recently, because other projects, such as the upgrading of the West Coast Main Line, have assumed a higher priority and will consume vast amounts of money, schemes such as later phases of EROS have been shelved and the mechanical signalbox, often controlling a route by Absolute Block (AB) signalling, will remain a convenient and cost-effective method of signalling secondary routes for a few more years. An excellent example of this is the largely AB-signalled line between Plymouth and Penzance, which for years has been a candidate for resignalling. It will now remain as it is although the signalboxes will be painted both inside and out!

Because of the economics of railway operations, a surprisingly large number of signalboxes remain. This book looks at some of the survivors, concentrating in the main on those opened before about 1960. Some are well-maintained, good-looking structures doing the same job as when the railway companies built them in the nineteenth century. Some are sadly showing their age and look incongruously over some weedy remnant of a once vital siding or station. A few are no longer part of the present railway system but continue to play a useful role as a shop or a tourist office or even a greenhouse. All, however, are reminders of a time past when railways were an essential part of Britain's life and carried goods and passengers reliably and frequently between our villages, towns and cities.

This book can be regarded as a companion to my earlier book, *Signals and Signalboxes of Great Britain*, published by Sutton in 1998. Since there is a gap of a few months between the submission of a manuscript and the appearance of a book, it represents, as far as I can tell, the situation on 1 January 2000.

Unlike the first volume, which looked at signalboxes according to the British Rail regions and then sub-divided them within the regions according to the company that built the 'box, the present book looks at signalling within the appropriate Railtrack zone irrespective of the origin of the structure. Finally this is, once again, a selection of the surviving signalboxes. I regret that I have been unable to cover certain areas such as the North Wales Coast fully. I particularly regret that in this book, no Scottish 'boxes are mentioned – perhaps next time.

RECENT CLOSURES

Photographed from the Brewery, this shows Brewery Sidings signalbox. Here, the Up and Down Goods connecting lines from Miles Platting Junction joined the lines between Manchester Victoria and Oldham or Rochdale. Opened by the Lancashire and Yorkshire Railway (L and YR) in 1894, Brewery Sidings 'box seemed in very good order. It was, however, closed in August 1998 as part of the Manchester Victoria resignalling scheme (MVAIR) that saw the closure of eight other boxes including Miles Platting Station Junction, Collyhurst Street and Philips Park Nos 1 and 2. (*19 May 1998; DJH*)

Philips Park No. 2 signalbox was located some 2.2 miles from Manchester Victoria on the Up West curve-side of the Ardwick Branch. It used to work under AB regulations with Baguley Fold Junction (about 2.5 miles from Victoria on the Down side of the Ashton Branch) and Philips Park No. 1, on the line to Miles Platting. Philips Park No. 2 was a difficult 'box to photograph from the front. Opened in 1889 by the L and YR to a Railway Signalling Co. design, it had been visibly altered over the years. Philips Park No. 2 'box closed in mid-September 1998, together with Philips Park No. 1, Miles Platting Station Junction 'box and others, during the second stage of the MVAIR work. The lines that were controlled by these 'boxes under AB regulations are now worked by Manchester North signalbox (opened in August 1998 under stage 1 of MVAIR) under Track Circuit Block (TCB) regulations to 'boxes at Vitriol Works, Oldham, Baguley Fold Junction, and Ashburys. (*18 May 1998; DJH*)

Bridlington Quay Crossing signalbox closed on 7 February 1998. It had been on the line from Hull to Scarborough via Beverley and Bridlington. As this photograph shows, it was a fine-looking 'box. Apparently a North Eastern Railway Type S4 of 1911, it had a history of rebuilding. The original 'box was opened in 1878. In 1908 it was extended and the top rebuilt to the S4 design (a design adopted at the end of 1905 which remained standard for the NER and it successors). The S4 design had the four-panes-deep operating-floor windows and plain bargeboards that are obvious here. The base, particularly the locking-room window design, pre-dates the S4 design. The area is now controlled from a switch panel in the former Bridlington South signalbox (now renamed Bridlington). The level crossing is now controlled via CCTV. (*25 August 1996; DJH*)

This photograph, taken from Platform 2 at Shalford Station looking towards Chilworth, shows Shalford signalbox. Shalford is on the Redhill–Guildford line and the 'box was, as can be seen, about 41 miles from Charing Cross. A British Railways (Southern Region) Type 16, it was not unappealing. It was built of brick with a flat, overhanging concrete roof. Shalford 'box closed on 4 January 1999 when Guildford signalling centre became responsible for the area. (*28 September 1997; DJH*)

The gatebox at Bathley Lane crossing (122 miles and 77 chains from Kings Cross) closed on 1 February 1998. The crossing is now controlled by Carlton Gate 'box some 3 miles away. As a signalbox, it was opened in 1930 by the London North Eastern Railway (LNER). The design originated with the Great Northern Railway and was classified as a GNR Type 4b. Bathley Lane 'box was obviously much modified. (*15 May 1996; DJH*)

EAST ANGLIA ZONE

CAMBRIDGE–NEWMARKET–BURY ST EDMUNDS

Chippenham Junction signalbox is involved in three types of signalling. Absolute Block signalling is used on the section to Kennett, Tokenless Block on the Newmarket line to Dullingham and Track Circuit Block on the Ely line. In this shot of the inside of the cabin, the sixteen-lever McKenzie and Holland frame and the instrument shelf can be seen. The levers, most of which have been cut down indicating their adaption for power operation, are clearly identified. On the left-hand side of the shelf, the Cambridge signal box alarm can be seen. The power supply indicators for the colour light signals can be seen in the large black box further to the right while, on the right-hand side of the shelf, can be seen the instrument for the Absolute Block section to Kennett. The grey box labelled 'Dullingham' is the Tokenless Block. (*4 April 1997; DJH*)

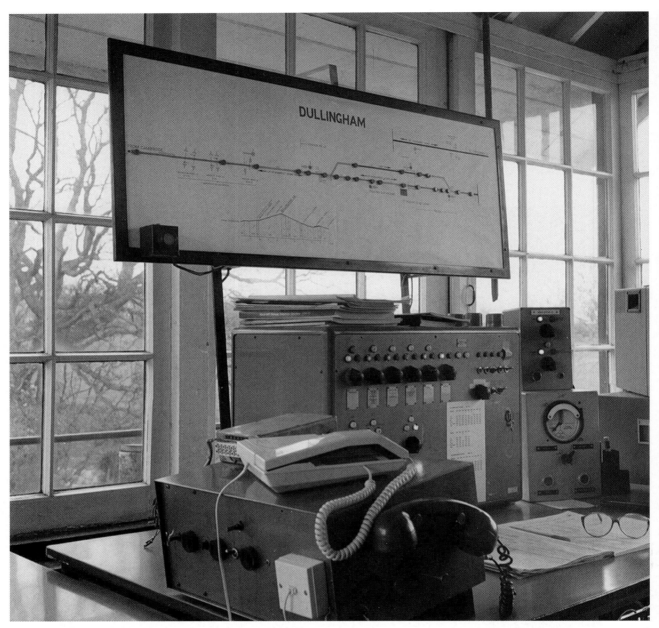

Dullingham signalbox is one of the last remaining Stevens-built Great Eastern Railway (GER) Type 4 'boxes. It opened in 1883 and, from the outside, looks like a well-maintained, classic Victorian 'box (see D.J. Hucknall, *Signals and Signalboxes of Great Britain*, 1998). Inside, the working area is dominated by equipment used for the Tokenless Block working of the Cambridge–Chippenham Junction line. Clearly shown in this photograph is the signalbox diagram. It depicts the single Up/Down Newmarket line with the crossings at Six Mile Bottom, Brinkley Road and Westley Road supervised by Cambridge, the loop at Dullingham and the single line to Chippenham Junction. (*April 1997: DJH*)

Brandon signalbox is 86.3 miles from Liverpool Street (via Clapton and Cambridge) on the Ely–Thetford section. Built by the LNER and opened in 1931, this fine-looking 'box stands by the side of the Down line, a short distance from the station, and dominates the level crossing and a difficult road junction. Classified as a Type 11c, it is not typical because of the extension at the station-end of the 'box. This is necessary to improve the signalman's view of the area. Brandon has a forty-lever GN Duplex frame and works with the 'boxes at Lakenheath and Thetford as part of the AB signalling between Shippea Hill and Wymondham. (*17 June 1999; DJH*)

Lakenheath signalbox is on the Down Norwich side of the Ely–Thetford line, some 82 miles and 44 chains from Liverpool Street. It works with Shippea Hill and Brandon signalboxes controlling the approximately 9-mile stretch of track according to AB regulations. Although a Great Eastern Type 4 'box, opened around 1885, Lakenheath is unusual because it was built not by McKenzie and Holland but by Saxby and Farmer. The difference is seen in the plain bargeboards although the fascia boards have the McK and H design. (*17 June 1999; DJH*)

Thetford station is on the Ely–Norwich line. The signalbox there is just beyond the end of the Down Norwich platform. Opened in 1883, it is an example of a Great Eastern Railway Type 4 built by McKenzie and Holland. The characteristics of McKenzie and Holland-built 'boxes of the period 1883–5 can be seen at Thetford. The operating-floor windows are four panes deep in sashes three panes across. The McK and H bargeboards are decorated in an interesting style which had newly been introduced. In addition to the signalbox, this photograph shows the Up Home signal, split to ensure that its indication will not be obscured by the footbridge linking the Up and Down platforms. (*17 June 1999; DJH*)

Opposite top: McKenzie and Holland had annual signalling contracts (including signalboxes) with the GER during the periods 1876–8 and again in 1882. (From 1886, the GER instituted further changes to its contract-awarding procedure.) The signalbox at Eccles Road was built by the company. It was opened in 1883 and is classified as a GER Type 4/McK and H. Built of brick, it has an overhanging gabled roof with cockscomb ridge tiles. The bargeboards and fascia have the relatively simple decoration which was to be seen on McKenzie and Holland 'boxes until 1890. Eccles Road signalbox is on the Up side of the Norwich–Brandon line and, in addition to control of the level crossing, works with Harling Road and Attleborough 'boxes as part of the AB signalling of the line. (*17 June 1999: DJH*)

Opposite, bottom: The Up and Down platforms at Attleborough station are separated by a road. Taken from the Up Thetford platform, this shows the signalbox, the level crossing gates and the Down platform. The signalbox is, like several others on the line, a typical McKenzie and Holland-built Great Eastern Railway Type 4, opened in 1883. This design has been described above. Attleborough signalbox works AB regulations with Eccles Road (3.75 miles to the west) and Spooner Row (3.10 miles to the east). (*19 June 1999; DJH*)

4

Harling Road signalbox was built by McKenzie and Holland and opened in 1883. Classified as a Great Eastern Railway Type 4, it controls the level crossing and works with Thetford and Eccles Road under AB regulations. (*17 June 1999; DJH*)

Spelbrook signalbox is a McKenzie and Holland/Great Eastern Railway Type 7 timber 'box, opened in 1898. It is 28.2 miles from Liverpool Street via Clapton between Broxbourne Junction and Bishop's Stortford. The neat, white-painted 'box oversees a level crossing with conventional gates. Although it retains several features of the Type 7s (three panes × three panes front windows, beaded fascia and bargeboards) the end windows by the entrance have been replaced. The LNER nameboard still remains. (*24 October 1999; DJH*)

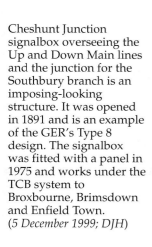

Cheshunt Junction signalbox overseeing the Up and Down Main lines and the junction for the Southbury branch is an imposing-looking structure. It was opened in 1891 and is an example of the GER's Type 8 design. The signalbox was fitted with a panel in 1975 and works under the TCB system to Broxbourne, Brimsdown and Enfield Town. (*5 December 1999; DJH*)

The signalbox on St Margaret's station is a GER Type 7, opened in 1887. A relatively large 'box (with a 56-lever McKenzie and Holland frame), it originally controlled the Hertford and Buntingford branch signals and points (the station once had a nameboard stating 'St Margaret's for Stanstead Abbotts change for Buntingford line') as well as the level crossing at the station. Today, its main function is that of a gate 'box. The signalbox is made of timber and the typical McK and H decoration can be seen on the bargeboards. The outside balcony for the operating-floor windows and its two stovepipes were removed some thirty years ago, however. (*5 December 1999; DJH*)

The existing GER Type 7 signalbox at Hertford East opened on 27 February 1888. It replaced one that controlled the approach to the original Hertford station. It contained thirty-six levers when first opened but the frame was expanded to forty-five levers when Hertford Junction 'box was closed. It is an excellent example of a McKenzie and Holland Type 7. (*5 December 1999; DJH*)

GREAT WESTERN ZONE

PENZANCE–PLYMOUTH

Roskear Junction signalbox is now the only one remaining in the Camborne/Redruth area. It works with the 'boxes at St Erth and Truro on the Penzance–Plymouth line. It was opened in about 1895 and controls a level crossing on Roskear Road near Camborne station. As its name indicates, however, it was also responsible for a long-gone branch line which left the main line and served the North Roskear mine. It is a GWR Type 5 and has most of the features of such 'boxes. It is not particularly eye-catching; the nearby dark-grey overbridge, the protective metal screens on the windows and the obvious alterations to the ridge of the roof make this a rather unappealing structure. (*June 1998; DJH*)

A type 60 locomotive No. 60023 pauses by the signalbox on the Up side of the island platform at Par with its load of china clay. The original signalbox was opened in about 1879 but its size was almost doubled in 1893. Par remains a fairly busy station and the outer face of the island platform is used for the single line branch to Newquay. This can be seen curving away to the right, rising at 1 in 100 to join lines coming from Par Harbour and Fowey. The bracket signals for the Branch and the Branch movements are at the end of the outer face of the platform. (*1 September 1999; DJH*)

Opposite: The Down Branch start signal at Par station (8 yards from the signalbox) dominates this photograph. To the right, three type 47 locomotives (*Resolute, Isle of Iona* and *Atlantic College*) pass the station on the Up line from St Blazey. (*1 September 1999; DJH*)

Par signalbox (281 miles 67 chains from Paddington) was originally 17ft 3in in length and, it is estimated, dated from the late 1870s. The 'box was lengthened to 38ft in 1893. It is suggested (P. Kay, *Signalling Atlas*, 1997) that the break in the line of window sills (below the edge of the left-hand whitened window in this photograph) indicates the extent of the new work. The signalbox continues to be altered. The vertical boarding which was used between the brick base and the working-level windows has been replaced and is now horizontal and the roof no longer has its ventilator and chimney. (*6 June 1998; DJH*)

The signalbox at St Blazey is a Great Western Railway Type 7d, opened on 25 June 1908 to replace an earlier structure. It is situated at the southern end of what was St Blazey station. To the left of the 'box in this view are the sidings and through sidings to Par Harbour. Several years earlier, the lines leading to the locomotive shed passed behind the 'box. The lines leading to Par station run in front of the signalbox. As can be seen, the Type 7 'boxes were made of brick and had hipped roofs and large eaves brackets. The Type 7ds had an additional locking-room window at the entrance end of the 'box. St Blazey signalbox is entered through the door marked 'Private' and has internal stairs. (*September 1998; DJH*)

A detailed view of the Par end of St Blazey 'box shows the decorative eaves brackets and the sliding 'three up–two down' windows. This end of the 'box was once used as an office for the yard foreman/wagon controller and an extension was located where the structure to the left now stands. (*1998; DJH*)

Side elevation of Church Stretton signalbox.

Church Stretton signalbox is one of seven surviving London North Western/Great Western joint 'boxes on the Shrewsbury–Hereford section. It is a square cabin with a brick base and relatively small operating-floor windows and was opened in about 1887. Church Stretton 'box is normally unmanned and signals are left in the 'off' position. In this photograph taken from the station, the Up Main inner home signal with a sighting board can be seen. In the distance, just beyond the overbridge, Church Stretton cabin is visible. (*October 1998; DJH*)

The signalbox at Marsh Brook (the name on the 'box although Railtrack prefers Marshbrook) guards a level crossing on a minor road leading from the A49. It dates from 1872 and is another example of a LNW/GW joint 'box. The line directly in front of the cabin is the Down Main and that nearest the camera is the Up Main. The signals controlling these lines at Marsh Brook are simple. Each has one distant and one stop signal, the former being a colour light. (*October 1998; DJH*)

A wind- and rain-lashed Bromfield signalbox is seen in this photograph. A further example of an LNW/GW joint Type 1 'box, it was opened in 1873. Just behind the structure are buildings belonging to Ludlow racecourse to which the crossing leads. In common with many crossings on this line, Bromfield's gates were replaced with lifting barriers in 1976. (*October 1998; DJH*)

The signalbox at Craven Arms (Craven Arms Crossing, formerly Long Lane Crossing) is an undistinguished-looking, grey-painted, timber structure dating from 1947. The gabled roof appears to be made of corrugated asbestos. It has several functions. With Marsh Brook and Onibury, it supervises a stretch of the Shrewsbury–Hereford line, a goods loop, the level crossing and, since the end of June 1986, the points and signals giving access to the Central Wales Line. (*October 1998; DJH*)

Tram Inn signalbox is one of the twenty-five that control the line from Gresty Lane No. 1 'box in Crewe to Little Mill Junction near Pontypool. This is the longest uninterrupted stretch of AB signalling on Railtrack. This photograph shows the end elevation of Tram Inn 'box seen from the south. Opened in 1894, it is classified as a Great Western Type 5, a design used from 1889 to 1897. It was apparently built on the brick base (Flemish bond) of the original signalbox. Over the years, modifications have taken place to the 'box – remnants of the finials can be seen and the horizontal weather boarding remains but the windows have been significantly altered. The level crossing gates at Tram Inn were replaced by lifting barriers in January 1974. (*24 September 1997; DJH*)

The signalbox at Pontrilas dates from 1880 when the Golden Valley Railway to Hay and the GWR agreed on how the GVR's customers were to be dealt with at the GWR's station at Pontrilas. As part of the agreement, the GWR undertook to make track alterations and other work including a new junction with the GVR and rearrangment of the goods yard. Additional signalling was supplied by McKenzie and Holland and included a new three-arm bracket signal and this 'box. At Pontrilas, the line from Hereford to Abergavenny and the south is built on an embankment. This photograph, taken from the rear of the McK and H Type 3 all-timber 'box shows that it is built on top of an under line bridge that crosses a track which used to lead to a wood alcohol factory. Some of the embankment retaining wall, which had to be partly rebuilt in the 1880 work, is also clearly seen. (*September 1997; DJH*)

As this side elevation shows, Abergavenny signalbox is a good-looking structure. It is set by the side of the track south of the railway station. It is a timber 'box with horizontal boarding which is painted off-white and contrasts pleasantly with the white structural members. Opened in 1934, it is classified as a Great Western Type 28b. It has a gable roof with four ridge vents. The locking-room windows are large and 3 panes deep. The 'box is fitted with a 52-lever, Great Western VT3 frame. It also has a hot-box indicator which receives information from a detector 6 miles to the south that checks the axles of northbound trains. (*September 1997; DJH*)

The extensive goods sidings and associated facilities that lay to the north and east of Shrub Hill station were inexorably removed in the 1960s and 1970s to leave a relatively basic layout. This undated photograph, although technically poor, shows Worcester Tunnel Junction signalbox in relation to the complex trackwork that existed prior to the 1960s. Behind the solitary brakevan is the London Yard and beyond that the sidings and facilities that served Shrub Hill goods shed. The complex of track between the water storage tank and the track with the locomotive led to the wagon repair shops. During 1972, a resignalling scheme was proposed which would have been concentrated on Tunnel Junction signalbox with colour light signalling and track circuiting between Tunnel Junction and Norton Junction and also Henwick. This was later abandoned. (*DJH Collection*)

Worcester Tunnel Junction's signals nos 39 (the smaller) and 17 are located some 55 yards from the 'box. No. 17 is the Down Main Home and No. 39 is the 'Engine Shed' Starting signal. The Down direction is to Droitwich Spa and Tunnel Junction signalbox works under AB regulations to Droitwich. (*27 July 1999; DJH*)

Tunnel Junction signalbox's Down Droitwich Starter, 388 yards from the 'box on the 'Droitwich Loop' to Foregate Street station, is repeated 271 yards from the 'box. Taken from what had been the Goods Engine Shed, this shows the banner repeater in the 'off' position. The finial on the repeater is identical to those on the lower quadrant signals. (*27 July 1999; DJH*)

Henwick signalbox was built by McKenzie and Holland and opened about 1875. It was enlarged by the GWR in 1897. It had a 25-lever GW frame fitted at this time. It oversees the level crossing on Henwick Road in Worcester and, since 1973, it has supervised the crossovers between the Birmingham line (the Droitwich loop – the former Up line) and the Oxford line to and from Shrub Hill (the former Down line) regulating trains across the junctions. Both lines are now worked as bi-directional single lines under Acceptance Lever Block Regulations to Tunnel Junction and Shrub Hill. AB working takes over on the double line toward Newland East and Malvern Wells. (*28 May 1997; DJH*)

Photographed from the former coal yard at the rear of Henwick 'box, the 1897 modifications can still be seen in the brickwork to the left of the centre pole. The roof of the enlarged 'box has several characteristics of the Type 7a design which appeared at the time of the modifications. For example, the hipped roof has terracotta finials, the eaves brackets are large and shaped and a shortened brick chimney is apparent. (*28 May 1997; DJH*)

Some of the levers and block instruments at Newland East Signalbox are shown here. The frame, a GW VT3, originally had thirty-three levers but, as can be seen, many are now redundant. Workings between Henwick and Newland East require that all Down trains are offered to Newland East after being accepted by Henwick. It is the duty of Newland East to provide routing information – Up trains taking the main line are distinguished from Branch trains by replacing the usual Entering Section bell code with 2-3-4. (*14 April 1999; DJH*)

Opposite, top: Newland East Signalbox was opened in 1900 and is beginning to show its 100-years' age. It is classified (P. Kay, *Signalling Atlas and Signalbox Directory*, 1997) as a Great Western Railway Type 7a. This type of 'box appeared in 1896 and Newland East has many of the accepted features – it is a brick-built 'box with a hippped roof with lead flashing on the hips and ridge tiles. The remnants of the terracotta finials can also be seen. The 'three up – two down' windows are also typical, as are the segmented arches over the locking-room windows. (*14 April 1999; DJH*)

Opposite, bottom: Malvern Wells signalbox works with Newland East and Ledbury 'boxes. Opened in 1919, it is classified as a Great Western Railway Type 7d (P. Kay, *Signalling Atlas and Signalbox Directory*, 1997). The 'box is built of brick (Flemish bond) and has a hipped roof. Type 7 signalboxes began to appear in 1896 and were widely used. Unlike the earlier Type 7s, Malvern Wells signalbox has ridge tiles and hip hooks. Two types of roof ventilator are fitted to the present 'box. Behind the current nameboard, the location and fixing points of the original can be seen. (*14 April 1999; DJH*)

Part of the frame and block shelf in Malvern Wells 'box is shown here. Clearly visible are the signalling bell and TB apparatus labelled 'Ledbury' and the block indicator and bell for Newland East. The original forty-lever frame is a Great Western VT3, installed in 1919. (*14 April 1999; DJH*)

The signalman at Malvern Wells signalbox fills in the Train Register. Through the window, the line leading to Colwall Tunnel and Ledbury can be seen. (*14 April 1999; DJH*)

A view of the inside of the signalbox at Worcester Shrub Hill station, looking away from the station. The track diagram and parts of the block shelf and the 84-lever GW5 frame, installed in 1935 when the 'box was new, can be seen. There is still an impressive number of working levers. Those shown here are from No. 20 (Down Up Main Facing–Branch), on the extreme left, to No. 84 (Down Main Distant) at the far end. Shrub Hill station 'box controls the routes from Tunnel Junction, Henwick and Norton. It also controls the southern access to the through sidings and the 'Engine Shed'. (*27 July 1999; DJH*)

A further view inside Worcester Shrub Hill station signalbox looking towards the station. The levers shown here are numbered from 64 (Disc at GF3 points) to No. 2 (Up Main Home). (*27 July 1999; DJH*)

A view from the road bridge showing Norton Junction and the signalbox. The single track diverging to the left is the Main Line to Evesham and Oxford. The right-hand pair of tracks are the Branch Line towards Abbotswood Junction and Gloucester and Bristol. The junction is in its 'normal' state with the line set for the route along the Down main line from Oxford towards Worcester. (*14 April 1999; DJH*)

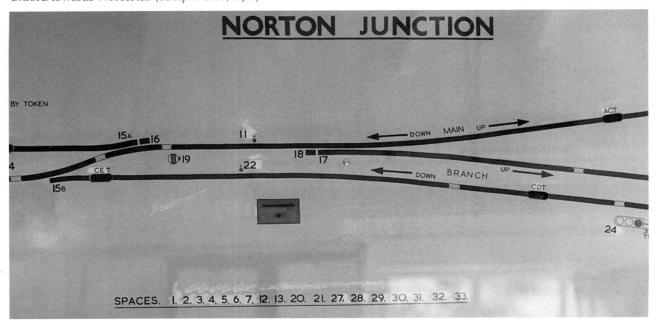

This photograph shows part of the track diagram inside Norton Junction signalbox (NJ). Electric Key Token (EKT) working is used between Norton Junction and Moreton-in-Marsh. An NJ–Evesham token can be issued at Norton Junction Signalbox (Instrument No. 376, Tyer and Co.) or from an auxiliary instrument at Shrub Hill station. Other signalling methods at NJ are AB to Worcester and TCB to Gloucester. (*27 July 1999; DJH*)

Some signals at Norton Junction have paraffin-lamp illumination. To show whether the lamps are lit or not, NJ has lamp indicators. This example is located on the block shelf in NJ and is cased in a light brown, polished, wooden box. The indication 'lamp in' reassures the signalman. (*27 July 1999; DJH*)

An interior view of Norton Junction signalbox, showing the signal levers, the block shelf and part of the keyboard used to communicate with Gloucester. The frame at Norton Junction was originally a 33-lever GW 3 bar HT but the frame for levers 27–33 and 1–7 has been removed. Of the levers clearly visible in this view, lever 22 controls the Down detonators, lever 23 is for the Down Main Starting Signal, 24 is the Down Branch Home, 25 is the Down Main Home and 26 the Down Main Distant. (*27 July 1999; DJH*)

Opposite: The signalman at Norton Junction gives a key token to the driver of a train which has come down the Main line from the direction of Evesham and is proceeding towards Worcester. EKT working is used between Norton Junction and Evesham and the former box has a Token instrument. To minimise delays in the service by token collection at NJ, there are two auxiliary Token instruments at Shrub Hill station, which can release or accept tokens. (*27 July 1999; DJH*)

An end elevation of the signalbox at Moreton-in-Marsh looking in the direction of Oxford. A GWR Type 4b, the 'box opened in 1883. It works under Absolute Block regulations with the signalbox at Ascott-under-Wychwood and with Key Token working with Evesham signalbox. (*5 January 1997; DJH*)

Like the 'box at Moreton-in-Marsh, that at Ascott-under-Wychwood is a Great Western Railway Type 4b, dating from 1883 when the Oxford–Worcester line was interlocked. Ascott signalbox works with TCB regulations to Oxford and under AB regulations to Moreton-in-Marsh. (*5 January 1997; DJH*)

The decline in railway activity at Banbury has been marked. Once, operations were controlled by four 'boxes – Banbury North, Banbury South, Banbury Junction and Ironstone Branch. The town also had, until the late 1960s, a busy locomotive shed which was opened in October 1908, about the same time as Banbury South 'box which controlled traffic to and from the depot. Banbury South 'box, seen in this view from the road/path that led down to the motive power depot, is a Great Western Railway Type 7d. It has a GW VT 5 frame which had eighty-seven levers when fitted in 1944. This was reduced to sixty-six levers in 1992, when a panel was fitted to control activities in the Anyho Junction area. The 'box now works under AB regulations to Banbury North and TCB with Marylebone IECC on the Chilterns and Oxford route. (*12 August 1999; DJH*)

Banbury North signalbox, seen here from the old Daventry Road overbridge, is a Great Western Railway Type 7b, opened in 1900. Among other duties, it used to control the entrance/exit to the large Hump Yard situated opposite the 'box. The Type 7 design appeared in 1896 and its characteristics are clearly seen with Banbury North. Built of brick, it has a hipped roof with large, decorative eaves brackets and iron hip hooks. With the Type 7s, the 'three up – two down' patterns windows appeared. At the top of the 'box stairs at Banbury North, the door leads to an internal porch with, and just visible through the end windows here, a second door to the right leading to the operating floor. (*12 August 1999; DJH*)

The 'box at Bentley Heath Crossing is good-looking and well maintained. It oversees a level crossing on the former Didcot and Chester line of the Great Western Railway, some 119 miles and 43 chains from Paddington. About 1 mile to the south is Knowle and Dorridge station. Classified as a GWR Type 28b, the 'box is made of timber with horizontal boarding. The 'three up – two down' windows give good visibility over the railway lines and the crossing and sliding sections from the corner posts and the central vertical support give additional ventilation.

Opposite: The former Greaves Siding signalbox stands out-of-use on the Up side of the former Didcot and Chester line, on the section controlled by Fenny Compton and Leamington Spa. It was opened in 1918 and is a Type 7d. It stands opposite sidings that were once used by Blue Circle Cement Co. The sidings are no longer used and are dismantled. (27 *March 1998; DJH*)

The GWR Type 11 signalbox at Yeovil Pen Mill was opened in 1937. It works with the 'boxes at Yeovil Junction, Westbury and Dorchester. (*31 March 1995; DJH*)

The signalbox at Maiden Newton stands forlornly out-of-use. It is a Great Western Railway Type 7d, dating from 1921. It was built as a replacement for the old signalbox which stood on the Down platform. Maiden Newton has seen busier days. In the late 1950s, for example, the traffic was such that the 'box was open from 5.45am on Mondays to 10.50pm on Sundays. (*24 October 1998; DJH*)

Oddingley 'box has no frame. It oversees the crossing of the former Midland Railway Gloucester–Birmingham line by a narrow road leading down to a farm. The line itself is worked by Gloucester and Saltley power signalboxes. Classified as a Midland Railway Type 3a, it was opened in 1908. It is built from standard MR 10ft panels bolted to solid-looking corner posts. At the front, the sash windows are made up of two sections, one of which slides over the other. The roof is hipped and is topped with a finial. Oddingley box's enamelled nameplate is discreetly mounted above the door. (*2 December 1997; DJH*)

Puxton and Worle 'box is a Great Western Type 7d, opened around 1916 to replace an earlier structure. The box measures 25ft by 11ft. It stands adjacent to a level crossing on a minor road. In January 1972, it was reduced from a signalbox to a Ground Frame for the level crossing and, in December of the same year, the gates were replaced by lifting barriers and the lever frame by an Individual Function Switch (IFS) panel. As can be seen, Puxton and Worle is in an awful state, tied together by scaffolding poles and braced with planks of wood. (*30 June 1997; DJH*)

Left: At the time of this photograph, Colthrop Crossing 'box was named Colthrop Siding G.F. (which stands for Ground Frame). A GWR Type 7c, it is situated on the Berks and Hants line between Midgham and Thatcham some 48 miles and 75 chains from Paddington. It was opened in 1912 as Calthorpe Crossing (R.A. Cooke, *Atlas of the Great Western Railway 1947*, Wild Swan Publications, Didcot, 1988) and acquired its present name in July 1999. (*6 April 1995; DJH*)

Below: Blakedown signalbox is on the former Oxford, Worcester and Wolverhampton Railway's line some 138 miles and 1122 yards from Paddington. Shown here is the GWR's cast nameplate on the front of the 1888 'box, still retaining its former name of 'Churchill and Blakedown' although with some careful overpainting. (*12 January 1997; DJH*)

LONDON NORTH EASTERN ZONE

RETFORD–GAINSBOROUGH–BARNETBY–BROCKLESBY

Seen here, Retford Thrumpton signalbox was built by the Manchester, Sheffield and Lincolnshire Railway (MSLR) and was opened in about 1889. In the early summer of 1965, Thrumpton was converted to a power box with a route-setting panel. This conversion coincided with the completion of the 'dive-under' which replaced the flat rail crossing of the East Coast Main Line by the Sheffield–Grimsby Line and resulted in the closure of six signalboxes (Welham Road, Gringley Road, Ordsall Crossing, Whisker Hill, Rushey Sidings and Checker House). (*26 November 1995; DJH*)

Northorpe station was situated between Gainsborough and Brigg on the line to Barnetby. The station closed in 1955 but the signalbox remains, overseeing the crossing with the Gainsborough–Kirton Lindsey road. Here the setting sun illuminates the flaking paintwork of the signalbox. The 'box was built by the Railway Signal Company for the MSLR in 1886 and shows the former's characteristic curve-and-spike bargeboard decoration. (*2 May 1998; DJH*)

The relief signalman climbs the steps to Ulceby South Junction signalbox (UJ). In this photograph, taken from the end of the Down platform, the line diverging to the left behind the 'box is the bi-directional line to Haborough Junction. The Down Immingham line to Brocklesby is not visible. UJ is a Great Central Railway Type 5 'box and was opened in 1910. The frame was supplied by McKenzie and Holland and, additionally, UJ has a panel, fitted in 1988, to control the Haborough area. The timber 'box is typical of a GC5. It has a gabled roof, relatively simple bargeboards, prominent finials and a gable-end window/ventilator consisting of 2 × 2 glass panes. The steps lead to a landing and the entrance, to the side of which is a toilet. When this photograph was taken, the 'box was in a good state of repair. It retained its LNER nameboard. (*2 July 1995; DJH*)

Near Barnetby le Wold, the chalk ridge that runs roughly north–south between the clay vale drained by the River Ancholme and the coastal plain of Lincolnshire dipped below 30 metres (The Barnetby Gap). This provided engineers building the line between Grimsby and Brigg with a fairly easy route. As Grimsby and Scunthorpe grew, so did the importance of Barnetby. Barnetby East signalbox is a Great Central Railway Type 5 dating from 1914. It works AB to Wrawby Junction to the west and Brocklesby Junction to the east. The buff-coloured wooden signalbox is shown here with its associated signals. A train is passing the 'box on the Down main line. (2 July 1995; DJH)

Stallingborough signalbox dates from 1884 and was opened by the Manchester, Sheffield and Lincolnshire Railway. Reflecting its origins, the 'box location continues to be given as 104.9 miles from Manchester London Road via Woodhead. Classified as an MSLR Type 2, it has survived in a reasonably unmodified form. Typical characteristics are its construction of battened boarding with the latter set diagonally at the gable ends. In the gable there is an opening window (2×2 panes). The windows are 3ft 6in deep with a horizontal glazing bar. Its bargeboards and finials are also typical. (31 May 1999; DJH)

The end elevation of Stallingborough signalbox from the Down main side of the station. Part of the conventional crossing gate can also be seen. The nameboard under the window – black lettering on white background – is typical of British Railways' mid-1960s style. (*31 May 1999; DJH*)

The rail system in the Port of Immingham is controlled by three signalboxes – Reception Sidings, Immingham East Junction and West Junction. All three date from 1912, the year of opening of the port by the Great Central Railway, and were required to control the 170 miles of railway within the port's confines. Reception Sidings 'box is shown here. In spite of its appearance, it is a GC Type 5 all-timber structure. It faces the Up and Down main lines which run between Humber Road Junction and Immingham East Junction and serve the EW and S sidings and depot. The brickwork is a protective casing and was built around both the 'box and the small building to the left that houses pneumatic equipment to operate the semaphore signals. It was installed by the LNER as a method of reducing the vulnerability of all-timber signalboxes to bomb damage in the Second World War. Standing on land owned by Associated British Ports, Reception Sidings is painted light blue and white rather than the usual grey. (*30 May 1999; DJH*)

Immingham West Junction signalbox stands in the fork between the lines serving North Killingholme Cargo terminal and the Western Jetty. With vegetation encroaching on three sides, the 'box has an incongruous look, seeming to have little connection with the railway it serves. Opened in 1912 together with Reception Sidings signalbox, it is a Great Central Railway Type 5 and, as with that 'box, Immingham West Junction cabin has had its base reinforced. When new, it controlled a triangular layout of lines but in the mid-1970s when the line was altered, the signalling frame was removed and replaced by an IFS panel. (*30 May 1999; DJH*)

A quiet period at High Street signalbox, Lincoln. Through the windows, the signalman can be seen relaxing. The barrier for the High Street crossing (one of the busiest in Britain) is raised and, beyond the 'box, Platforms 7 and 8 at Lincoln station are almost deserted. High Street 'box, a GN Type 1, was opened in 1874 by the Great Northern Railway. Together with Pelham Street Junction signalbox, 440 yards away at the opposite end of the station, it controls the semaphore signals in the station area. (*23 January 1998; DJH*)

Looking superb in spite of its 127 years, East Holmes signalbox in Lincoln was built by the Great Northern Railway and is doing much the same job as it did when opened in 1873. It is involved in one of the shortest sections of Absolute Block signalling on Railtrack – the 242 yards between High Street and East Holmes. The 'box is, unusually, an all-timber example of the GN Type 1 built in the 1870s and 1880s. It has a gabled roof, large finials and highly ornate bargeboards. The sliding windows are three panes deep and there is also glazing down to the operating floor. (*23 January 1998; DJH*)

An example of an LNER Type 11b, Saxilby signalbox is on the Lincoln–Gainsborough former GN/GE Joint line. The Type 11s were the usual 'boxes erected in the southern area of the LNER during the period 1924–41. They had brick bases, gabled roofs with plain bargeboards and concrete lintels over the locking-room windows and door. They also had rear frames (see the position of the signalman above). Differentiation between the sub-types of these 'boxes appears to be made in the number of panes of glass in the height of the working-area windows. As a Type 11b, Saxilby 'box has three. The nameboard on Saxilby 'box is noteworthy: it is probably the British Railways' original and is dark blue enamel with white letters. Also worth a comment is the boarded panel in the centre front of the 'box. Behind this was the stove to heat the working area and the repair on the roof indicates where the stovepipe protruded. (*23 January 1998; DJH*)

The next signalbox beyond Saxilby in the direction of Gainsborough and Doncaster is Stow Park. It oversees a level crossing on the A1500 and is part of the AB signalling section from Saxilby to Beckingham. Stow Park is classified as a GN Type 1/Bessacarr design signalbox and was built as part of a contract awarded to Saxby and Farmer in 1876 to equip the Stow Park–Gainsborough–Bessacarr line. Compared to East Holmes, another GN Type 1, for example, Stow Park is markedly different. Its base is made of panelled brick and it has a toilet on the landing at the entrance. Minor differences include the shorter finials and unperforated bargeboards. (*2 May 1998; DJH*)

Gainsborough Lea Road signalbox is located at the Lincoln end of the Up platform at Lea Road station. It works block sections with Stow Park (approximately 4.88 miles to the east) and Gainsborough Trent Junction (approximately 0.65 miles to the west) 'boxes. Its opening dates from about the time of the Saxby and Farmer contract (see Stow Park, above). It is regarded as a GNR Type 1 structure and shows clearly the vertical boarding, the expected number of gable-end windows and the three-panes-deep operating-floor windows, extending from a little above floor level up to the eaves. The bargeboard pattern and finials are typical of the Bessacarr 'boxes. Unusually, however, Lea Road 'box is made of timber. (*19 November 1994; DJH*)

Finningley gate-box is on the Lincoln–Doncaster line, approximately 5 miles from Doncaster station. Like most of the 'boxes on this line, it dates from 1877. (*9 July 1996; DJH*)

Many of the surviving Great Northern Type 1 'boxes seem to have changed very little since their opening. Such an example is at Allington Junction where a GN Type 1, opened in 1875, oversees a level crossing and the divergence of the Nottingham–Boston and Nottingham–Grantham lines. The 'box is built of brick (laid in English bond) and the gabled roof has a substantial overhang. The working-level windows are four panes deep and the bargeboards are particularly ornate. Allington Junction signalbox (108.9 miles from Kings Cross) works AB signalling with Bottesford West Junction and Barkston East Junction on the Boston line and TCB with Doncaster on the Grantham line. (*29 December 1997; DJH*)

Proof, if it was needed, of the survival of some significant artefacts from Britain's railway history. This cast-iron notice warning potential trespassers and dated 1898 was photographed three years ago near a level crossing in Nottinghamshire. (Other examples can be seen elsewhere in this book, see page 59.) (*29 December 1997; DJH*)

The signalbox at Bottesford West Junction was built by the GNR in 1876 in connection with the GN/LNW joint line junctions. A GN Type 1, the box is located adjacent to the Up line, almost exactly 114 miles from Kings Cross. Relatively unaltered with its LNER name board at eaves' level, multi-paned windows, ornate bargeboards and brick chimney, it is nevertheless showing more evidence of wear-and-tear than its neighbour at Allington Junction. Large areas of brickwork have been rather crudely repointed and the paintwork is flaking and falling off. (*29 December 1997; DJH*)

Opened around 1873, Ancaster signalbox stands on the Up side of the former Great Northern Railway's Boston, Sleaford and Midland Counties Line. One of the more venerable versions of the GNR's Type 1 'box, it has a steeply pitched roof topped with the remains of ornate ridge tiles. Through the windows, some of the handles of the thirty-lever Saxby and Farmer rocker frame can be seen. Ancaster works under AB regulations with Barkston East Junction to the west and Rauceby to the east. (*8 July 1996; DJH*)

Almost 120 years old, Sleaford East signalbox, seen through typical urban clutter, is another variant of the Great Northern Railway's Type 1. It stands some 120.73 miles from Kings Cross via Grantham, overlooking the level crossing at the east end of the station. Sleaford East works under AB regulations to Sleaford West, some 550 yards away, and under TCB regulations to Heckington on the Boston line and to Sleaford South on the Spalding line. (*28 May 1995; DJH*)

Not a frequently photographed signalbox, Norton West stands at one of the corners of the Norton triangle which links lines to and from Darlington and Northallerton with those from Hartlepool and Ferryhill. This end elevation was taken looking in the direction of Norton South. The 'box is classified as a North Eastern Railway Southern Division Type 4 and dates from about 1920. The S4 style was adopted by the NER in 1905 and was used into the 1930s. Photographically, a drawback of Norton West and some others in the area is the necessity for steel shutters to protect the windows when the 'boxes are not in use. On the day when this shot was taken, about three-quarters of the operating-floor windows at the front of the box were shuttered in this way. (*August 1999; DJH*)

Norton-on-Tees signalbox is a North Eastern Railway Central Division Type 2a, dating from 1897. It stands next to the level crossing on Station Road and, like the 'box at Billingham, is a very tall structure. It is built of brick with a hipped roof and its operating-floor windows are four panes deep, giving good visilbity and illumination for the signalman. (*August 1999; DJH*)

The signalbox at Billingham-on-Tees towers over its surroundings. Dating from 1904, it is classified as a North Eastern Railway Central Division Type 2a. It is part of the AB signalling system which controls the Durham Coast line. It also works with Belasis Lane signalbox on the former Clarence Railway which serves the petrochemical activities of Teesside. Two notable features shown here are the extensions from the working level, one at least of which would improve the view of Billingham Junction, and the unusual crossing barriers which seem only to be found in the former North Eastern region. (*August 1999; DJH*)

These splitting signals stand outside the signalbox at Billingham-on-Tees. The taller one refers to the former NER's Stockton and Hartlepool line between Norton-on-Tees East and Hartlepool. The lower signal refers to the former Clarence Railway line that branches off the Hartlepool line at Billingham Junction. (*August 1999; DJH*)

Urlay Nook signalbox is 7.5 miles from Darlington. It was built in 1896 and contained a sixteen-lever frame at the front of the 'box. Subsequently, some very significant alterations were made. For example, the steps and door are now on the opposite side of the 'box to their original position. Major signalling alterations took place in 1943 and the 'box was extended at its west end to accommodate a new 41-lever frame which was located at the back of the 'box. Nowadays, most of Urlay Nook's levers are spares. The siding with the nearby chemical works has gone and no regular freight traffic passes the 'box anymore. Since 1991, Urlay Nook works to Tyneside IECC with a VDU-type train describer and to Bowesfield by TCB. (*17 May 1996; DJH*)

Belasis Lane signalbox is 1 mile and 4 chains from Billingham-on-Tees 'box and is on the former Clarence Railway. The junctions of the Up and Down lines can be seen near the 'box. It was opened by the LNER in 1929, although its design was based on the North Eastern Railway's Southern Division Type 4. Belasis Lane 'box looks a little the worse for wear. The brick extension at the entrance is heavily shored up, the roof is showing its seventy years and the nameboards given to the 'box over the years are peeling and decaying. (*August 1999; DJH*)

Greatham signalbox is at a level crossing on a dead-end road some distance from the village. It is a North Eastern Railway Northern Division Type 1 'box, opened in 1889. It is on the Stockton–Hartlepool line where the sections are Billingham-on-Tees to Greatham and Greatham to Cliff House. As the latter is now switched out, except for the once or twice weekly nuclear flask train serving Hartlepool power station, the section is generally Greatham to Stranton. Greatham 'box is typical N1. It is plain brick with a hipped roof. However, the operating windows are three panes deep and the small locking-room windows have stone lintels. Immediately on the left-hand side of the level crossing are the remains of Greatham station. (*4 August 1999; DJH*)

Wylam is on the Newcastle–Carlisle line and has a superb signalbox. Painted in a striking red/brown and cream it is one of only three overhead 'boxes existing in Britain (the other two are at Hexham and Canterbury West). Wylam 'box was built about 1897 and is supported on an iron gantry set into brick walls. Taken from the Up platform, this photograph shows these features together with the lattice footbridge and the Down platform beyond the crossing. (*6 August 1999; DJH*)

After the amalgamation of the Newcastle and Carlisle and the North Eastern Railways in 1862, the former became part of the Northern division of the NER. There followed a decade of construction and rebuilding to accommodate the growing traffic on the line, particularly coal. The signalbox at Prudhoe dates from this time. It is a tall 'box, probably to oversee, among other things, the rail link to Prudhoe Colliery. It is brick-built and classified as a Northern Division Type 1. It has a hipped roof and operating-floor windows two panes deep with sliding sections two panes wide. Over the following thirty or so years after the building of Prudhoe 'box, traffic of all types increased on the Newcastle–Carlisle line to the point that the 'box was extended in 1908. In this photograph, the change in brickwork marking the work can be clearly seen. Other additions and changes are also visible. (*6 August 1999; DJH*)

The diversity of 'boxes classified as NER Northern Division Type 1 can be seen if this photograph of Haydon Bridge 'box is compared to that of Prudhoe. Situated at the western end of the station's Up platform, it is built in stone, and was opened in 1877. It has a hipped roof fitted with a roof vent typical of the NER. The two-panes deep, two-panes wide sliding windows have an additional row on the corner of the 'box overlooking the level crossing. Haydon Bridge 'box and its gated crossing look slightly incongruous in its surrounding. This is reinforced by a nearby cast-iron sign, contemporary with the 'box, on which the North Eastern Railway warns of the consequence of trespassing. (*6 August 1999; DJH*)

The former NER Northern Division had several examples of overhead gantry boxes (including Corbridge to the east of Hexham) but now only those at Wylam and Hexham remain. The present 'box at Hexham was one of two that controlled rail traffic there. There was once a West signalbox located at the Carlisle end of the Up platform. The gantry at Hexham spans the Up and Down Carlisle lines but the 'box itself lies above the freight sidings. Built in 1918, it would

have overlooked lines to the loading dock (where the line of timber carriers can be seen), the engine shed (approximately where the buildings are), cattle dock sidings and, still visible beyond the Up line fence, several other sidings. (*6 August 1999; DJH*)

The signalbox at Hebden Bridge is 23.6 miles from Manchester Victoria. It stands just to the east of the station's Up Main platform. It works under AB regulations with Milner Royd Junction (about 5½ miles to the east) and, to the west, is a fringe 'box to Preston PSB. Hebden Bridge signalbox dates from 1891. It was built by the L and YR (but prefabricated in the latter's Horwich Works) to a design originating with the Railway Signal Co. The RSC design was very similar to one initially produced by the Gloucester Wagon Co. The latter is perpetuated in the gable-end windows (2 × 2 panes), the locking-room windows (2 × 2) and the operating-floor windows with lower panes. (*1 October 1996; DJH*)

Opposite: The former Lancashire and Yorkshire Railway's line ran from Goose Hill Junction near Normanton (50.4 miles from Manchester Victoria via Rochdale) and followed the Calder Valley as a convenient route through the Pennines to Manchester. Some 4.9 miles to the west from Goose Hill Junction is Horbury Junction. There, 45 miles from Manchester Victoria, the branch line to Barnsley diverges. Horbury Junction signalbox, seen here looking from the west, stands close to an overbridge carrying the M1. It is basically an LNW Type 5, opened in 1927. The L and YR amalgamated with the LNWR in 1922 and, thereafter, the LNW Type 5 became the norm for new 'boxes on the former L and Y lines. Horbury Junction works TCB with Healey Mills and Leeds 'boxes on the Calder Valley line and with AB regulations to Wooley Coal sidings (since 1996, a relay room) on the Barnsley branch. (*16 March 1997; DJH*)

The signalbox at Malton is a well-kept structure located on the Up side of the York–Scarborough line, 21.4 miles from York. Classified as a North Eastern Railway Southern Division Type 1a, it is built of stone and has a gabled roof with a substantial overhang. As is usual with this type of 'box, the operating-floor windows are three panes deep with one sliding and one fixed sash. The glazing is in short sections, separated, in this case, by stone pillars. An unusual feature of the windows here is the corner window (2 panes × 3 panes) which gives an additional view of the level crossing. Malton 'box was fitted with an IFS panel in 1966. It works under AB regulations to Kirkham Abbey and Weaverthorpe. (*25 August 1996; DJH*)

Seamer East signalbox (13 miles and 17 chains from York) is a North Eastern Railway Southern Division Type 4, dating from 1910. It has its original McKenzie and Holland frame with thirty-five levers (see below). Presently, it works under AB regulations with Falsgrave and Seamer West but the latter, structurally, is in dire straits. It seems likely that, in the near future, the route between Hunmanby and Seamer will be resignalled and control of the area (including the present functions of the 'boxes at Seamer West, Filey and Hunmanby and the gate 'boxes at Cayton, Lebberston and Gristhorpe) will be taken over by a refurbished Seamer East. (*25 August 1996; DJH*)

An interior view of Seamer East signalbox showing the McKenzie and Holland frame and levers. (*25 August 1996; DJH*)

Eastfield signalbox was opened in the 1890s (estimated 1893). It is classified as a Great Northern Railway Type 1, a fairly broad category covering the GNR 'boxes of the 1870s, 1880s and 1890s. All had pitched roofs (some quite steep), large finials and decorative bargeboards. Vertical boarding at the gable ends and glazing almost down to operating-floor level were other features. Eastfield 'box once had a window in the gable above the nameboard. (*15 June 1997; DJH*)

Opposite: The block section between Bedlington North and Bedlington South signalboxes is, at 242 yards, one of the shortest sections of AB signalling on Railtrack. Here the North signalbox is seen from the crossing near the South signalbox. On the right-hand side of the railway tracks are the remains of Bedlington station which had only one through platform. The lines curving away to the left lead to Morpeth. Just visible in front of the 'box are the lines leading to West Sleekburn Junction. In its heyday, Bedlington North had to deal with large numbers of coal trains (40–50 per day to West Sleekburn) as well as passenger and parcel trains. It also dealt with three sets of level crossing gates. (*August 1997; DJH*)

Bedlington North signalbox is classified as a North Eastern Railway Northern Division Type 4. Such structures had brick bases, laid in so-called English-garden-wall bond, and gabled roofs. They were introduced in the late 1900s and 1910s and Bedlington North is an example from 1912. A close-up of the entrance to Bedlington North is shown here. The two Bedlington 'boxes have always worked closely together. In days of heavy traffic, there was an extra block bell between the cabins so that South 'box could indicate the direction of a train (Morpeth or Newbiggin) to the North cabin. Similarly, a train from Morpeth would, on passing Choppington, indicate whether it was proceeding down the branch or going straight through to Bedlington. This was passed to Bedlington South. (*August 1997; DJH*)

A close-up view of the non-door end of Bedlington South signalbox shows very clearly the English-garden-wall bond brickwork and the former LNER nameboard. (*August 1997; DJH*)

Dating from around 1899, Shirebrook Junction signalbox stands at the point where the line to Warsop Junction and Welbeck Colliery diverges from the line to Shirebrook East Junction. The 'box is classified as a modified Midland Railway Type 2 (Signalling Study Group, *The Signal Box*, 1986). It is a timber 'box with two locking-room windows at the non-door end. (*17 May 1996; DJH*)

LONDON NORTH WESTERN ZONE

HELLIFIELD–SETTLE JUNCTION–CARLISLE

Hellifield was once a junction of some importance. It was where the Lancashire and Yorkshire Railway's line to Blackburn joined the Midland Railway's Settle Junction–Leeds line. It had an engine shed (formerly the Midland Railway's shed), a carriage shed and an exchange sidings for the LYR/MR traffic. There were also two signalboxes – Hellifield North Junction and South Junction. Architecturally, the station is a gem which almost decayed to the point of no return. Hellifield South Junction signalbox (231.2 miles from St Pancras) still remains. Built by the Midland Railway, it came into use in 1911. It oversees the divergence of the line to Clitheroe and Blackburn from the lines from Settle Junction to Skipton and the South. It works with Absolute Block signalling to Settle Junction and Horrocksford Junction and Track Circuit Block signalling towards Skipton. (*16 March 1997; DJH*)

Inside Settle Junction signalbox showing part of the lever frame and the block shelf. The 'box itself was built in 1913 and contained a Midland Railway 25-lever tappet frame. In 1960, this was replaced by a standard 1943 pattern frame with 31 levers. In this photograph a table on which a pair of binoculars stands can be seen. This is the table which was hit by a railbolt during the 1979 china clay train derailment (see D.J. Hucknall, *Signals and Signalboxes of Great Britain*, 1998).

Garsdale station is on the Settle–Carlisle line just over 3 miles from the summit at Ais Gill. The signalbox stands on the Down platform. Not normally manned, it was built by the Midland Railway in 1910 and brought into use on 10 July of that year as Hawes Junction. It is classified as a Type 4c and is 30ft × 10ft 6in × 8ft (see Anderson and Fox, *Structures and Stations of the Settle and Carlisle Railway*, 1986). In this photograph, looking north from the Up platform, the line curves away towards Moorcock viaduct and tunnel. The signals that can be seen are permanently pulled 'off' in the deserted signalbox. (*30 December 1997; DJH*)

Strictly, the BR (LMR) standard Type 15 signalbox at Kirkby Stephen should not be included in this selection. The original 1894 former Midland Railway 'box, known officially as Kirkby Stephen (Midland), was closed on 27 October 1974 and replaced by the structure shown. A flimsy excuse for its inclusion could be that the present 'box contains a twenty-lever standard LMS pattern frame of 1943 recovered from Kendal signalbox. When Garsdale signalbox is switched out, the block sections for Kirkby Stephen are 18 miles to Blea Moor and 11 miles to Appleby North. (*30 December 1997; DJH*)

Appleby formerly had two signalboxes – Appleby West and Appleby North Junction. A third, Midland Junction signalbox, was on the former NER Penrith–Kirkby Stephen–Darlington line. The original North Junction 'box (opened in 1890) was located just beyond the end of the Down platform at the Carlisle end of the station. It was destroyed by fire on 4 June 1951. The replacement for North Junction 'box, seen here, is located on the other side of Settle–Carlisle line where the lines used to diverge towards the Eden Valley line. It is a wooden, LMS-design structure and originally contained a standard Railway Executive Committee (REC) twenty-lever frame, extended to twenty-one levers. On the closure of Appleby West signalbox in July 1973, the frame was extended again to twenty-five levers. (*30 December 1997; DJH*)

Located 284.7 miles from St Pancras, the present signalbox at Culgaith stands by the Up side of the Settle–Carlisle line adjacent to the level crossing. Opened on 4 October 1908, it replaced an earlier structure removed during the Midland Railways resignalling programme. It works with Kirkby Thore and Low House Crossing 'boxes using AB signalling. Classified as a Midland Railway Type 4a structure, it is a relatively small 'box with a sixteen-lever tappet frame. It appears to be in reasonable condition, its hipped roof retaining both finials. The double locking-room windows are in the Midland Railway style but the working-level windows are obviously replacements. (*30 December 1997; DJH*)

Askam station, opened on 1 April 1868, is on the original Furness Railway (FR) line of 1846. Relatively little has changed since its construction. The Paley and Austin-designed buildings, dating from 1877, are intact while the stone signalbox, a Furness Railway Type 2 opened on 30 October 1890, is essentially unaltered. Obviously, lifting barriers have replaced the original closing gates. (*11 February 1998; DJH*)

End elevation of Foxfield 'box.

Opposite, bottom: In 1858, the Furness Railway, extending from Kirkby in the south, and the Whitehaven and Furness Junction Railway, coming from the north, were linked at Foxfield. The station at Foxfield, however, dates from 1879. An island platform was built, one side of which served the line to Whitehaven while the other side was used by trains on the Coniston branch. The signalbox, added to the end of the platform and once attached to the station buildings, is estimated to date from this time (P. Kay, *Signalling Atlas and Signal Box Directory*, 1997), although there is some doubt about this. The timber 'box is unlike the usual FR brick or stone 'boxes. The frame dates from 1909, which coincides with a recorded 'extension' to the box. (*12 February 1998; DJH*)

The signalbox at Bootle, classified as a Furness Type 1, dates from about 1874 and is typical of the FR's country signal boxes (see also Drigg). The base is solidly built of large, even, stone blocks and is slightly larger than the superstructure. The windows are relatively large and there are upper lights. The hipped roof is in a reasonably good condition and carries the name of the 'box above the eaves, a practice adopted by the LMS for its Furness structures. Bootle cabin has a fourteen-lever standard LMS frame, fitted in 1977, and originally located in the 'box at Nethertown. (*12 February 1998; DJH*)

The present signalbox at Silecroft was opened in 1923 when the original wooden structure on the Whitehaven side of the of the level crossing was closed. The later signalbox was built on the south side of the level crossing and on the opposite side of the station. According to *The Signal Box, a pictorial history and guide to designs*, The Signal Study Group, 1986, Silecroft is a Furness Railway Type 4. Notable are the panelled brick base and the absence of finials on the hipped roof. The signalling frame was built by the Railway Signalling Co. and has been reduced to fifteen levers. (*12 February 1998; DJH*)

Together with the signalboxes at Bootle and Ravenglass, that at Drigg is one of the oldest Furness Railway 'boxes known. Dating from about the mid-1870s, it is classified as an FR Type 1. It has a stone base typical of the early 'boxes. The main windows have no horizontal glazing bar and above them are upper lights which are typical of Saxby and Farmer's early signalbox designs. (*12 February 1998; DJH*)

Salwick signalbox opened in 1889 when the Lancashire and Yorkshire Railway's line between Preston and Kirkham was widened from two to four tracks. The fast lines have now been lifted as the overgrown area between the 'box and the present lines shows. The 'box still retains its original name – Salwick No. 2 (No. 1 was at the Preston end of the Down goods loop). It is a fringe 'box to Preston PSB; the Salwick–Preston section is controlled by colour lights. (*28 January 1998; DJH*)

Kirkham North Junction signalbox dates from 1903 when the Lancashire and Yorkshire Railway changed the track layout and signalling in the area to accommodate a third route from Blackpool. The 'box was especially busy in the 1930s and the early post-Second World War years at the time of the 'Illuminations' at Blackpool when up to 600 trains/24 hours could, reportedly, be handled. In 1975, Kirkham North Junction 'box was officially renamed 'Kirkham' after the cabin at Kirkham and Wesham station was closed. The original name still appears at the entrance end, however. From the outside, Kirkham signalbox looks impressive. Its roof bargeboards and finials remain in good condition. Even the locking-room windows are intact. The lower row of the operating-floor windows have, however, been blocked off. Inside, changes have been made over the years and the frame has been reduced to fifty-seven levers. (*29 September 1998; DJH*)

Opposite: Until 1971, Poulton-le-Fylde had five signalboxes (Nos 1–5). Poulton Nos 1 and 2 were at the Preston end of the station, Nos 4 and 5 were on the Blackpool and Fleetwood lines, respectively. Poulton No. 3 has survived. Opened in 1896 by the L and YR, it is located some 88 yards from Poulton-le-Fylde Junction where the line to Burn Naze joins the line to Blackpool North. (*9 April 1999; H.C. Hillmer*)

Only four former Cheshire Line Committee (CLC) signalboxes remain – Mouldsworth Junction, Plumley West, Mobberley and Northenden Junction. Mouldsworth Junction is on the CLC's Altrincham and Chester line where the Helsby branch to West Cheshire Junction turned off. This branch has been closed since 1991 when the West Cheshire Junction box was destroyed by vandals. Essentially, Mouldsworth Junction signalbox is a much-modified CLC Type 1a. The Type 1s were made of timber but the base of the cabin was rebuilt in 1989 with a brick surround. Although the hipped roof and fixed upper lights are typical and the operating-floor windows have a sliding section near the corner posts, the latter are no longer three panes deep and show evidence of relatively recent alteration. (*20 November 1998; DJH*)

Opposite, top: In addition to being one of the four surviving CLC 'boxes, Mobberley is the only example of a CLC Type 1b. Some 11.9 miles from the former Manchester Central station, it is on the CLC's Altrincham and Chester line. Opened in 1886, it is built of timber with vertical boarding. It is cream in colour with brown main members. Although there are no upper lights, the three-panes-deep operating-floor windows with sliding sashes near the corner posts are typical (see Signalling Study Group, *The Signal Box*, 1986). The nameboard is missing but there is an excellent example of the CLC style at Northenden Junction (see D.J. Hucknall, *Signals and Signalboxes of Great Britain*, 1998). (*8 September 1996; DJH*)

Opposite, bottom: Helsby Junction signalbox was opened in 1900. It is built on the island platform at Helsby station. In this photograph, the 'box is seen from Platform 1. The lines in the foreground are the Up and Down Warrington lines between Chester and Frodsham. The 'box, which has nameboards on the front and at both ends, is an example of an LNWR Type 4 with a gabled roof and bargeboards set directly over the gable-end boarding. The red finials are also set into the boarding. It has a 45-lever LNW tumbler frame and works Absolute Block regulations to Mickle Trafford. In 1992, its control was extended to include the section handled by Helsby West Cheshire Junction on the destruction of the latter 'box. (*20 November 1998; DJH*)

A view of Helsby Junction signalbox from Platform 4 showing the rear of the 'box. The lines in the foreground are the Up and Down lines between Hooton and Helsby. The route is controlled by AB regulations throughout. (*20 November 1998; DJH*)

Opposite: Frodsham Junction signalbox stands on a steep embankment. It is an LNWR Type 5 opened in 1912 as a replacement for an earlier cabin. The Type 5 'boxes were characterised by a roof overhang which was significant compared to the Type 4s, allowing more conventional bargeboards and finials (although Frodsham Junction 'box has lost three out of its four ball-and-spike finials). They also had 6ft, sliding sash windows. This signalbox works AB regulations with Helsby Junction and Norton signalboxes; the north-bound line, which is the only line in use from Frodsham Junction to Halton Junction and which passes behind the 'box, is also worked by AB signalling. Notable in this view of the rear of Frodsham Junction 'box is the LNWR sign indicating catch points. This probably dates from its opening. (*31 March 1999; DJH*)

Crosfields Crossing signalbox is 11 miles and 770 yards from Skelton Junction on the former Timperley and Garston line. Opened in 1913, the 'box is classified as an LNWR Type 4 with some non-standard features. It works under AB regulations with Arpley Junction and Litton's Mill Crossing signalbox. (The latter is 220 yards away.) This line is kept open at the moment to control the movement of traffic to and from Fiddler's Ferry power station. (*12 January 2000; DJH*)

This view of the inside of Crosfields Crossing signalbox shows the block shelf and signal levers. The frame is an LNWR Tumbler frame of 1913 and has eighteen levers. Now, most of the levers are out of use but those working at present are Nos 3 and 12 (Home signals), No. 17 (Release Lever for Crosfield's Crossing ground frame) and No. 18 (Barrier control lever). (*12 January 2000; DJH*)

Inside Crosfields Crossing (*12 January 2000; DJH*).

Litton's Mill Crossing signalbox is small and undistinguished and stands in the shadow of the now-disused mill. An LNWR Type 4, it opened in 1890 and works with Crosfields Crossing and Monks Siding to control the line serving Fiddler's Ferry power station. In addition, the 'box oversees the crossing to Litton's Mill, just on the other side of the line. (*12 January 2000; DJH*)

Some 550 yards from Litton's Mill Crossing stands Monks Siding signalbox. A LNWR Type 3, it was opened in 1875. Monks Siding works with Litton's Mill Crossing and Fiddler's Ferry power station 'box. (*24 July 1997; J.C. Hillmer*)

A close-up of the entrance to Winsford signalbox, an LNWR Type 4 of 1897. The view clearly shows the bargeboards placed over the boarding of the 'box and the position of the finial, although the lower ball and spike are missing. The windows are protected by mesh to prevent damage from debris that might be raised by high-speed, passing trains. On 14 September 1997, Hartford Junction and Weaver Junction 'boxes closed and their areas of control were transferred to Winsford signalbox, using a newly-fitted panel. The Winsford area, however, continued to be worked using Winsford's 1897 LNWR frame. (*23 May 1997; DJH*)

Ashton Moss North Junction signalbox is 3.16 miles from Baguley Fold Junction 'box. It is a timber structure opened in 1911 by the Lancashire and Yorkshire Railway and built by that company at its Horwich works. When this photograph was taken, the 'box appeared to be in good condition. It works under Absolute Block regulations with Baguley Fold Junction and Stalybridge 'boxes. (*October 1996; DJH*)

Opposite: In 1960, there were sixteen signalboxes between Manchester Victoria and Stalybridge of which eight could be found within the 2.6 miles to Baguley Fold Junction 'box. Inevitable closure had reduced this number to three (Collyhurst Street, Miles Platting Station Junction and Philips Park No. 1) by 1998. On 15 September 1998, however, these three 'boxes were also closed (others in the area had closed that August) and the lines formerly controlled by them were worked by a new signalbox, Manchester North (opened in August 1998 at Salford Crescent Station) under TCB regulations to fringe 'boxes, one of which is Baguley Fold Junction signalbox. Baguley Fold Junction was opened 110 years ago for the Lancashire and Yorkshire Railway. It was built by the Railway Signal Co. and its characteristic bargeboards can be seen in this view. During the resignalling of 1998, Baguley Fold 'box lost its lever frame which was replace by a panel. (*18 May 1998; DJH*)

From Llandudno Junction on the Chester and Holyhead line, there is a branch to Llandudno. Some 1 mile and 16 chains down the Branch stands Deganwy station. Deganwy signalbox works under AB regulations with Llandudno and Llandudno Junction. It also oversees the level crossing at the Llandudno end of the station. It is an LNWR Type 5 'box with an eighteen-lever frame. (*January 1998; Michael McKenna*)

The signalman at Rainford Junction 'box near St Helens waits for the train from Kirkby. The section of line from Kirkby to Rainford Junction is worked under OTS (one-train working with staff) regulations. From Rainford Junction to Wigan Wallgate, AB regulations apply. Rainford Junction 'box is a hybrid. The Saxby and Farmer brick base dates from 1874. The upper part of the 'box dates from 1933 and is classified as an LMS Type 11c. (*21 June 1997; DJH*)

MIDLANDS ZONE

TAMWORTH–LICHFIELD–STAFFORD

In my opinion, the LNW 5 design has much more appeal than the Type 4. The overhang of the roof, the bargeboards and finials becoming more apparent, probably has a lot to do with its attractions. The Type 5 signalbox at Lichfield is an excellent example. It stands between the Up and Down Fast lines at Trent Valley station some 116.3 miles from Euston. Opened in 1911, it has a brick base (as did all Type 5s), slightly overhung by the working area. The light blue and cream woodwork at the time of this photograph makes the 'box stand out from its surroundings. Lichfield Trent Valley No. 1 works under Absolute Block regulations to Lichfield Trent Valley Junction 'box and under Track Circuit Block regulations with Hademore Crossing and Colwich. (*1 April 1997; DJH*)

A side elevation of Stafford No. 4 (SD 4) signalbox, an example of the British Railways (London Midland Region) Type 15 'boxes that were first introduced in 1954 and used until early 1985. They were prefabricated, standardised structures, maintaining the tradition of the LMS and the Midland Railway. SD 4, opened in 1960, is a long box, made up of seven wooden panels at the operating-floor level, on a brick base. An unusual feature is the small 'look-out' mid-way along the operating level. In the 1970s, SD 4 took over the work of four other 'boxes (Stafford Nos 1 and 2, Queensville and Milford, and Brocton). Its 105 levers now work the lines under Track Circuit Block regulations to Stafford No. 5, Penkridge on the Bushbury to Stafford line and Shugborough on the Trent Valley line. (*3 May 1998; DJH*)

Opposite: Entrance to Stafford No. 4 'box is via a steel staircase leading directly to the operating-frame door. Clearly seen here is the enamelled nameboard in the style of British Railways (LM Region) with white capital letters on a maroon background above the door. The brick base (laid in English bond) and the timber-panelled upper works are also apparent. (*3 May 1998; DJH*)

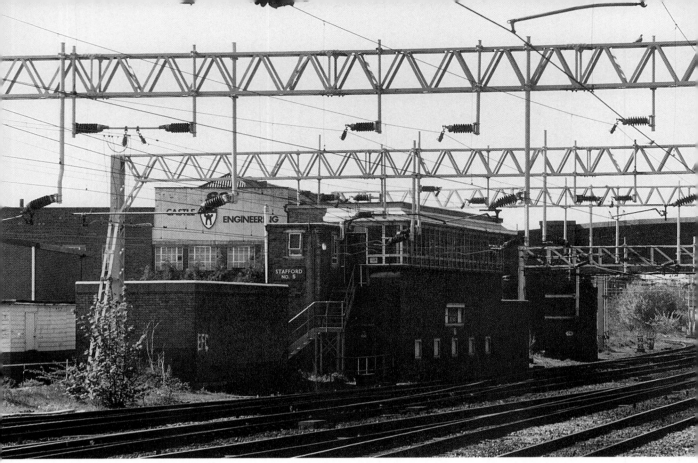

In the shade and almost obscured by the overhead wires, insulators and gantries, Stafford No. 5 (SD 5) signalbox stands at the north end of Stafford station. It was opened on 18 February 1952 and has 150 levers. An example of a London Midland region Type 14, it was built of brick at a time when signalboxes were architect-designed and had a certain amount of individuality. A significant feature of SD 5 is the extension at the entrance end of the 'box for the lavatory. When opened, the signalbox controlled the changed layout and colour light signalling that were necessary for the planned electrification of the lines from Euston to Birmingham, Liverpool and Manchester. Much of SD 5's work disappeared on the closure of the lines to Uttoxeter and Wellington and, compared to the smaller Stafford No. 4 'box, it is now relatively quiet. (*3 May 1998; DJH*)

Opposite: Lichfield Trent Valley station is on two levels, the higher-level platforms serving the South Staffordshire line. Taken from the Down Walsall platform at Trent Valley station, this shows Trent Valley Junction signalbox (Lichfield T.V. Jct as the nameboard indicates) on the Up side of the line approximately 18.2 miles from Dudley Junction. The 'box is a LNWR Type 4 opened in 1897. It works under AB regulations with Alrewas signalbox (approximately 4 miles to the east). (*1 April 1997; DJH*)

Alrewas signalbox is a London North Western Railway Type 4. It was opened in 1899. Although the gable roof and brickwork appeared to be in reasonable condition when this photograph was taken, the gable-end woodwork and window frames were in need of attention. Because some of the glazing on Type 4 'boxes was fixed, external walkways were provided to assist cleaning. At Alrewas, wooden guard rails have also been added. Just over a mile from Alrewas 'box, at Wichnor Junction, the Derby to Birmingham line joins the South Staffordshire line. The junction and the route to Derby is controlled using TCB by Derby PSB. (*? DJH*)

There are numerous examples of the prefabricated Midland Railway (*c.* 1870–1929) timber signal 'box which was in use for almost 60 years. Shown here, Lowdham 'box is a Type 2b, opened in 1896. The end windows and front operating-floor windows are consistent with the original MR design. Those at the non-door end are 3ft 6in deep, two panes × two panes. The operating-floor windows, 5ft 1in deep, are 2 panes wide × 3 panes deep. (*8 July 1995; DJH*)

Part of the 1902 Midland Railway frame at Fiskerton (12 miles and 46 chains from Nottingham London Road Junction). Fiskerton cabin is not a block post and most of the 16 levers are out of use and even partly dismantled. (*8 July 1995; DJH*)

The rather curious crossing gates at Rolleston are opened and closed by a gatekeeper rather than controlled by a gate box. The crossing lies just to the west of the station and, in this photograph, the gatekeeper, John Charlton, watches a train leaving Rolleston station in the direction of Nottingham. (*8 July 1995; DJH*)

Until recently, the boundary between the Midland and London North East zones of Railtrack lay to the east of Newark Castle station, approximately 0.6 miles from the signalbox. Now, for operational convenience, Newark Castle's signalbox will have been transferred to the control of the LNE zone. The signalbox, certainly at the time of this photograph, was an excellent example of the Midland Railway's neat timber cabins. Opened in 1912 and classified as a Type 4a, it retains almost all the expected features. The operating-floor windows are 4 panes across, sliding from the corner post. The walkway is typical of pre-1913 'boxes. The stovepipe emerging from the roof at the front shows that the 'box has a rear frame. (*8 July 1995; DJH*)

As with Newark Castle 'box, responsibility for the signalbox at Swinderby will now have been transferred to the LNE Zone of Railtrack. Previously, it was in the section of the Midland Zone that extended from just west of Collingham almost to Wrawby Junction. Unmistakably a Midland Railway signalbox, Swinderby is located on the Up side of the Nottingham–Lincoln line. Working under the TCB system with West Holmes 'box and Doncaster PSB, Swinderby is responsible for a section running from Collingham station to Hykeham station. It was opened in 1901 and is classified as a Midland Railway 3a. (*23 January 1998; DJH*)

Hinckley signalbox is 3 miles and 70 chains from Nuneaton South Junction on the Nuneaton–Leicester line. It is an LNWR Type 4, dating from 1894 and displays the usual features of such 'boxes. According to Banks (*The Birmingham to Leicester Line*, 1994), Hinckley signalbox caught fire on 14 January 1986, due to the malfunctioning of a newly installed stove. The 'box was re-opened within 48 hours of the fire. (*14 January 1996; DJH*)

Melton is on the present Nuneaton–Peterborough line, which is a continuation of the Nuneaton–Leicester line. Melton signalbox, opened in 1942 and classified as an LMS Type 11c, works under AB regulations with Frisby station 'box and Saxby Junction 'box. It is an unusual structure because of both its height and its overhang. It was designed to allow the signalman a good view of movements in the sidings directly in front and to the rear of the 'box. (*24 August 1996; DJH*)

SOUTHERN ZONE

SOUTH EAST

STROOD–PADDOCK WOOD (NORTH KENT LINE)

The line from Strood to Paddock Wood follows closely the course of the River Medway. The northerly part of the route, as far as Aylesford, runs through a built-up, industrialised area. South of Aylesford, the surroundings are much more pleasant. The signalbox at Cuxton overlooks a level crossing leading to and from the River Medway. It is a timber structure built by the South Eastern Railway (SER). It has light-blue painted sash windows, each with four panes of glass. The roof is hipped and made of corrugated asbestos. It works with Snodland, using Absolute Block signalling and with Dartford using Track Circuit Block signalling. (*10 August 1997; DJH*)

The present buildings, including the signalbox, and platforms at New Hythe, originate from 1939, when the electrification of this line north of Maidstone West was completed. Classified as a Southern Railway Type 13, this rather undistinguished 'box is situated at the north end of the platform serving the Up Maidstone line. The signalbox has a small frame (twenty levers) and works with the boxes at Snodland and Aylesford. (*10 August 1997; DJH*)

Opposite, top and bottom: Snodland signalbox stands by the side of the Up Maidstone line, separated from the railway station by a level crossing. It is a SER timber structure, opened in the 1870s, with typical SER horizontal boarding, sash windows and a hipped roof. Extending from the 'box is a lower structure which in the past housed a gate wheel for the level crossing gates. These were replaced in 1973. (*10 August 1997: DJH*)

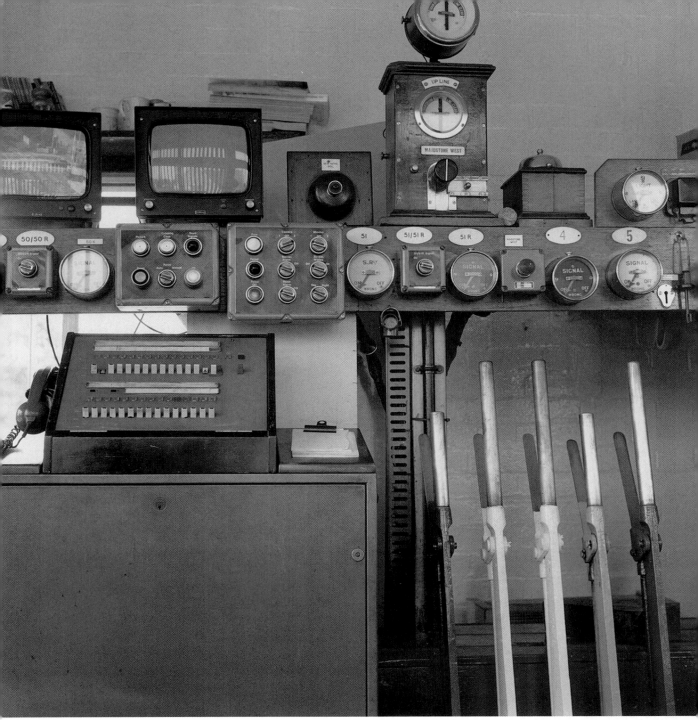

The instrument shelf, part of which is shown here, and the signal frame at Aylesford signalbox are located at the rear of the 'box. By the 1930s, this became normal practice for many of the railway companies. Aylesford's block shelf is quite cluttered and dominating this shot is the Southern Railway's three-position block instrument to work the section to Maidstone West and the TV monitors and controls for the Aylesford and Aylesford village level crossings. Both crossings have power-operated lifting barriers with emergency local control. (*10 August 1997; DJH*)

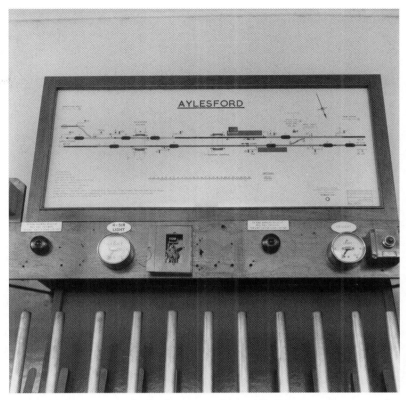

The framed and glazed diagram of the signals and the layout at Aylesford are seen here. All distances shown on the diagram are in yards from the centre of the 'box. For example, Aylesford Village crossing is 862 yards from the 'box. On the block shelf below the diagram, the light repeaters for signals 23 and 51R can be seen. (*10 August 1997; DJH*)

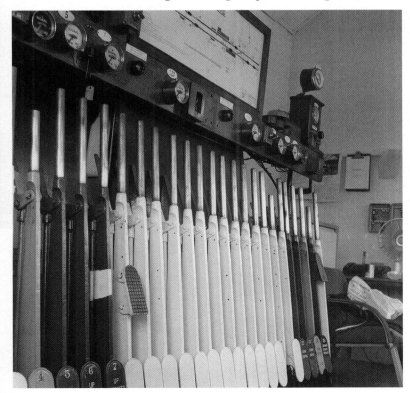

Wateringbury's signalman Jonathan Butson hurries down the signalbox steps to close the crossing gates to road traffic. The signalbox was designed by Saxby and Farmer and opened in 1893. Classified as a Type 12a of that company, it was of a design used in the period 1890–4. The 'box has a brick base and a working level that is horizontally boarded. The gabled roof has a significant overhang at the front and rear. Notable is the green and white enamelled nameboard typical of the Southern Railway. (*10 August 1997; DJH*)

Opposite, top: The Saxby and Farmer Type 12a signalbox which once overlooked the crossing at Yalding continues to survive but at some considerable distance away at Horsebridge station near Kings Sombourne in Hampshire. Horsebridge station was on the 'Sprat and Winkle' line until it was closed by Dr Beeching in 1965. The station was superbly restored in 1985 by its present owners and the former Yalding signalbox stands on the platform approximately where Horsebridge signalbox once stood. (*1998; DJH*)

Opposite, bottom: A view of the signalbox and crossing at East Farleigh. The South Eastern was the only British railway company to use the same design for signalboxes and station buildings in some locations. East Farleigh is a notable example. This practice was for cheapness rather than architectural harmony (*The Signal Box*, 1986). East Farleigh 'box was opened in 1892 and is predominantly made of horizontal, overlapping boards. The hipped roof is made of what appears to be corrugated asbestos. The windows are two panes deep and the end windows are wide open on a blistering August day. (*10 August 1997; DJH*)

Part of the block shelf and some of the lever handles inside the signalbox at Wateringbury. A Southern Railway standard three-wire, three-position block instrument, labelled 'East Farleigh', is visible. Repeaters for the signals can be seen along the front of the shelf. It was a warm afternoon at Wateringbury. The thermometer standing on the controller for Beltring level crossing barriers reads 90F. (*10 August 1997; DJH*)

Wye station is on the former South Eastern Railway's branch from Ashford to Ramsgate, some 60.4 miles from Charing Cross via Chelsfield. The signalbox, opened in 1893 and a typical Saxby and Farmer 'box of 1890–4, is located at the opposite end of the Up platform from the level crossing. Such structures (SER Type 12a) are built of horizontal overlapped timber boards and have large windows and a gabled roof. (*18 July 1999; DJH*)

The Down starter signal at the end of the Down platform at Wye and referred to in the caption below is shown in this view. (*18 July 1999; DJH*)

Opposite: Because of the footbridge connecting the platforms, the view of the Down starter signal on the platform end at Wye is significantly impaired. To assist the driver, a banner repeater is located in front of the overbridge. On the Southern Railway, the Sykes' electrical banner was adopted as standard (Pryer, *A Pictorial Record of Southern Signals*, 1977). The banner at Wye clearly shows the components – the block arm, pivoted in the centre, deflecting against a white background in a glass-fronted case. (*18 July 1999; DJH*)

Canterbury West signalbox is one of the three remaining overhead 'boxes in Britain (the other two are at Wylam and Hexham – see pages 57, 60–1). It seems excessively large (it contains a seventy-two-lever SECR standard frame) for the present truncated railway. Until 1979, however, Canterbury West had four running lines (two through lines and two serving the platforms) passing through the station. It also had various sidings and bays. Opened on 1 January 1929, the

'box replaced two others – Canterbury West No. 1 and No. 2. No. 1, which was situated at the west end of the station, was an elevated 'box and No. 2 also straddled a track. For a signalbox which was installed fairly recently in railway terms, there seems to be uncertainty about the 'box's history. A comment in the *Signalling Atlas and Signalbox Directory* (1997) states 'box and/or frame secondhand from Blackfriars Junction'. (*18 July 1999; DJH*)

The gate box at Sturry is a Saxby and Farmer Type 12a dating from 1893. It retains some of the features of the original design – the hipped roof, the two-panes-deep windows and the horizontal lapped boarding. Sturry is on a lengthy section of AB signalling between Canterbury West and Minster. (*18 July 1999; DJH*)

Approximately 6½ miles from Wye in the direction of Canterbury lies Chartham. The signalbox there is a small, well-preserved timber structure opened by the South Eastern Railway around 1880. The horizontal, overlapping boards are painted dark green and the hipped slate roof has lead flashings. (*18 July 1999; DJH*)

The railway from Faversham to Canterbury opened on 9 July 1860. At Canterbury East station (62 miles approximately from London Victoria via Hearne Hill), the most significant feature is the very tall signalbox at the end of the Down platform. It is an SECR 'box, dating from 1911. For such a relatively large structure, its frame (twenty-eight levers, LCDR) is fairly small, particularly as Canterbury East once had extensive goods sidings on both sides of the line. (*18 July 1999; DJH*)

SOUTH CENTRAL

GUILDFORD–REDHILL

The former Chilworth signalbox is situated at the Guildford end of the Down Reading platform at Chilworth Station. An RSC 'box built for the South Eastern Railway, it is now the home of Signal Music – Clarinet and Saxophone Tuition. (*28 September 1997; DJH*)

Opposite, top: An example of a Southern Railway's Type 11B, the signalbox at Reigate stands at the end of the platform on the Up Reading side of the line. Opened on 10 March 1929, it contains a twenty-four-lever Westinghouse A2 frame. Reigate 'box has some interesting features. Above the operating-floor windows are small, top-light windows and, above the top-lights on the end elevations, there is horizontal, panelled boarding. Below the central group of windows at the front of the 'box, the mounting for the British Railways nameboard remains. (*28 September 1997; DJH*)

Opposite, bottom: The signalbox at Farncombe oversees the level crossing at the west end of the station on the former Portsmouth Direct line. It dates from 1897 and is classified as a London South Western Railway Type 4. This design emerged in the mid-1890s and represented a significant departure from what had gone before; the design was used until the late 1920s. Farncombe is a typical Type 4. The operating-floor windows, unusual for contemporary design trends, were divided by a wide brick pillar. Although the glazing (2 panes × 2 panes windows) is close to the original pattern, the frames do not have curved tops anymore. Farncombe 'box does not have a frame, being fitted with individual function switches. (*9 January 2000; DJH*)

(GUILDFORD)–PORTSMOUTH

At the end of Platform 2 at Littlehaven station stands this odd structure which combines the functions of gate box and booking office. It was opened by the Southern Railway in 1938. Although this photograph was taken three years ago, the gates which protect the Rusper Road level crossing seem to belong to a quieter, pre-Second World War age. (*28 September 1997; DJH*)

Opposite, top: Haslemere signalbox looks superb. It stands on the station's Down platform, approximately 43 miles from Waterloo. An LSWR Type 4, it was opened in 1895. It works TCB with Farncombe and Petersfield. As with Farncombe, the operating-floor windows do not have curved framing at the top. They also appear to tilt, not slide. (*9 January 2000; DJH*)

Opposite, bottom: This view shows Petersfield signalbox from the Haslemere end of the Down platform. It is a very striking 'box. An LSWR Type 3, its operating floor is almost entirely glazed but the deep valancing obscures the upper lights. It controls, by TCB, a section of line of some 18 miles from about 1 mile south of Liphook almost to Havant. (*26 December 1996; DJH*)

Horsham signalbox was brought into use on 24 April 1938. It is a Southern Railways' Type 13, described as 'One of the most striking of all twentieth century 'box designs' (Signalling Study Group, *The Signal Box – A Pictorial History*, 1986). This fine 'box is barely discernible among the clutter of its surroundings. The lines running in front of the 'box and then diverging are the Branch to Three Bridges (curving to the right) and the main lines (diverging sharply to the left). (*28 September 1997; DJH*)

Described as 'probably the most historically-significant signalbox on the Railtrack system' (P. Kay, *The Railway Magazine*, 146, 39 (2000)), Billinghurst 'box is some 44.9 miles from London Bridge (via Redhill) and stands at the end of the Up platform. Although recorded as being opened in 1876, Kay regards this as an underestimate of its age. As a Saxby and Farmer Type 1, the design would not have been used in the mid-1870s and Kay suggests that the 'box was built in the 1860s and moved to Billingshurst. Since John Saxby holds such a significant place in railway signalling history, the only surviving example of his first standard 'box is obviously treasured by anyone with an interest in Britain's railway past. (*28 November 1999; DJH*)

Marchwood is on the line from Totton to Fawley which was opened by the Southern Railway in July 1920. The signalbox at Marchwood, opened in 1925, is merely a brick-built hut on the station platform. This photograph of the interior of the 'box shows many items of interest including some of the handles of the signal levers on the Stevens' frame, fitted in 1943, and the Tyer's block instrument, formerly at Eling but moved to Marchwood when the sidings to the military port were laid during the Second World War. Hanging above the windows are the single line tablets and, in front of the windows, is the desk with the train register, the signalbox clock and the noticeboard. (*5 March 1995; DJH*)

Some 146 yards from Marchwood signalbox in the direction of Totton are the splitting home signals for the Up/Down main line and the Down Main–Down Goods Loop (the lower signal). The signals show LSWR connections although the upper quadrant arms originate with the Southern Railway. The unused line in the foreground leads to a sand drag. On the extreme left, one of the automatic half barriers at Tavell's Lane Crossing can be seen. (*17 January 1999; DJH*)

A fine example of an LSWR splitting signal at Marchwood. The lattice dolls are typically positioned on either side of the main post. The higher of the upper quadrant arms is for the main line to Fawley. The lower signal is for the line leading to the reception/exchange siding for Marchwood Military Port. (*17 January 1999; DJH*)

South West

Bournemouth–Dorchester

A view of the signalbox at Bournemouth from what used to be the engine shed yard but is now, inevitably, a car park. It is a Southern Railway Type 11c 'box, opened on the 8 July 1928 to replace Bournemouth East and West 'boxes. The dimensions are 28ft 8in × 9ft 4in and the 'box is elevated some 24ft (it is above the platform canopy). It is fitted with a Westinghouse A2 frame with sixty levers. The structure is timber with a hipped roof. The operating-floor windows are in sections that are 2 panes × 2 panes. There are also glazed upper lights. (*DJH*)

(*Opposite*) An unusual view of a Westinghouse Brake and Signal Co. pattern ground disc signal that became standard on the Southern Railway. It is in the Bournemouth Traction and Rolling Stock Depot and is controlled by the Ground Frame (the former Bournemouth West Junction Signalbox – a superb example of an LSWR Type 3a (see Hucknall, *Signals and Signalboxes of Great Britain*, 1998)). This signal is externally illuminated and has no colour lights showing on the disc. (2 May 1997; DJH)

Bournemouth Carriage Sidings Ground Frame (formerly West Junction 'box until 1965) is a tall box in excellent condition. It is a Type 3a of the London South Western Railway, opened in 1888, with a contemporary Stevens frame (for views of which see Hucknall, *Signals and Signalboxes of Great Britain*, 1998). It is continuously manned and controls all movements at the Branksome end of Bournemouth Maintenance and Traincare depot. (*2 May 1997; DJH*)

There seems to be some doubt about the design and opening date of Wool signalbox. According to Kay (*Signalling Atlas and Signalbox Directory*, 1997), it is an LSWR Type 3b, opened about 1890. Pryer (*Signal Box Diagrams*, Vol. 2 *SR Lines in East Dorset*) and Jamieson (1997) suggest it is a Type 3c of 1878. It has, however, been considerably altered. The 'box stands at the Dorchester end of the Up Main Line platform some 125.9 miles from Waterloo and supervises the adjacent level crossing. Absolute Block regulations apply to Wareham and from Dorchester Junction (Moreton) in the Up direction. Track Circuit Block was introduced from Wool to Dorchester Junction on the Down line in June 1970. The original 'box was approximately 16ft × 10ft (elevated 8ft 3in) but was extended in 1988 to improve working conditions. Considerable alterations to the windows were also made. (*25 May 1995; DJH*)

At Honiton, there is a crossing loop on the singled stretch of the Exeter–Salisbury line between Pinhoe and Yeovil Junction. The signalbox at Honiton is located at the western end of the loop platform. Opened on 16 June 1957, it was one of several British Railways (Southern Region) 'boxes built on this line. Other examples remaining, but not necessarily in use, are at Sherborne and Gillingham. (*16 August 1996; DJH*)

Warnham signalbox (33.6 miles from Waterloo via Worcester Park) stands at the end of the Up platform on the Horsham–Dorking line next to Station Road level crossing. It is an example of a Saxby and Farmer Type 5 signalbox and was built for the London, Brighton and South Coast Railway. This design was widespread from 1876 to 1898 and Warnham (1877) is typical. It has a hipped roof, large eaves brackets, windows (two panes deep) with curved tops and upper lights. The brick base is laid in Flemish bond and is fitted with two four-paned locking-room windows. (*21 May 1995; DJH*)

The Down side, right-hand bracket gantry signal at Warnham is a Southern Region upper quadrant, built in the manner of the Southern Railway. The main post is made of old rails and the doll is of lattice construction to save weight. (*21 May 1995; DJH*)

AN IRISH EPILOGUE

James Mullen, the signalman, walks towards the level crossing at Woodlawn signal cabin to close the gates in preparation for the evening Galway–Dublin train. At Woodlawn, the main line is single and the line nearest the 'box actually serves a cattle dock. Until partition, Irish signalling followed British practice and Woodlawn cabin was opened around 1885 having been built according to an RSC design. The RSC influence can be clearly seen in the bargeboard decoration although the look of the 'box must have been considerably altered when it was rewindowed. Inside the 'box, the 1885 frame is clearly marked RSC, Liverpool. It has very few working levers now. (*8 October 1998; DJH*)

The RSC-designed signalbox opened for the former Midland Great Western Railway at Ballinasloe in 1891 is illuminated by the evening sun. Standing out spectacularly is the lower quadrant semaphore signal which is, like all Irish rail semaphore signals, painted a highly reflective orange-red to aid visibility. Ballinasloe 'box, on the Dublin–Galway line, has been rewindowed and its appearance must be very different to the original. (*7 October 1998; DJH*)

The signalbox at Athenry was opened in 1927 by the Great Southern and Western Railway (GS and W). It is a solid-looking 'box built on a stone base and overlooking the station (to the left of box), a level crossing and a now disused siding and loading dock. The crossing gates seem insubstantial when compared to those built by the British pre-grouping companies but there can be no doubt about their visibility. (*7 October 1998; DJH*)

BIBLIOGRAPHY

Allen, D., and Wolstenholmes, C.J., *A Pictorial Survey of London Midland Signalling*, OPC, Sparkford, 1996

Anderson, V.R., and Fox, G.K., *Structures and Stations of the Settle and Carlisle Railway*, OPC, Poole, 1986

Banks, C., *The Birmingham to Leicester Line*, OPC, Sparkford, 1994

Cooke, R.A., *Atlas of the Great Western Railway 1947*, Wild Swan Publications, Didcot, 1988

Cookson, P., and Fairline, J.E., *LNER Lines in the Yorkshire Ridings*, Challenger Publications, Oldham, 1995

Dent, D., *150 Years of the Hertford and Ware Railway*, The Rockingham Press, Ware, 1993

Hucknall, D.J., *Signals and Signalboxes of Great Britain*, Sutton Publishing, Stroud, 1998

Jamieson, M.A., 'Signalling on the Bournemouth–Weymouth Line, Pt. 2', *The Signalling Record*, 62, 1997, p. 38

Kay, P., *Signalling Atlas and Signalbox Directory, Great Britain and Ireland*, Peter Kay, Teignmouth, 1997

Maclean, A.A., *A Pictorial Record of LNER Constituent Signalling*, OPC, Oxford, 1983

McLoughlin, B., *Blackpool and the Fylde*, Silver Link Publishing, Wadenhoe, 1996

Norton, P.A., *Waterways and Railways to Warrington*, Cheshire Libraries and Museums, 1985

Potts, C.R., *An Historical Survey of Selected Great Western Stations*, Vol. 4, OPC, Poole, 1985

Pryer, G., *A Pictorial Record of Southern Signals*, OPC, Oxford, 1977

——, *Signal Box Diagrams of the Great Western and Southern Railways*, Vol. 2, *SR Lines in East Dorset*; Vol. 9, *Bournemouth to Southampton and Branches*; Vol. 14, *GWR Lines: Plymouth and East Cornwall*

Signalling Study Group, *The Signal Box – a pictorial history and guide to designs*, OPC, Poole, 1986

Smith, W.H., *The Golden Valley Railway*, Wild Swan Publications, Didcot, 1993

Webb, G.E.C., *The Railway Magazine*, 94, 307, 1948

Wells, J.A., *Blyth and Tyne Part. II: The Blyth and Tyne Branch 1874–1989*, Northumberland County Library, 1990

Whittle, G., *The Newcastle and Carlisle Railway*, David & Charles, Newton Abbot, 1979

Yonge, J., and Jacobs, G. (eds), *Railway Track Diagrams 2. England: East*, The Quail Map Co., Exeter, 1998

——, *Railway Track Diagrams – England South and London Underground*, The Quail Map Co., Exeter, 1994

INDEX